THE
HEAVENLY
VISION

WITNESS LEE

Living Stream Ministry
Anaheim, California

© 1997 Living Stream Ministry

First Edition, September 1997.

ISBN ISBN 0-87083-852-0

Published by

Living Stream Ministry
1853 W. Ball Road, Anaheim, CA 92804 U.S.A.
P. O. Box 2121, Anaheim, CA 92814 U.S.A.

Printed in the United States of America

97 98 99 00 01 02 / 9 8 7 6 5 4 3 2 1

CONTENTS

PREFACE

This book is composed of messages given by Brother Witness Lee in Los Angeles, California in the summer of 1965.

Chapter One

THE VISION OF CHRIST

Scripture Reading: Acts 26:19; Gal. 2:1-2a; Rom. 1:9a; 2:29; 2 Cor. 3:6

In Acts 26:19 the apostle Paul said, "I was not disobedient to the heavenly vision." In this book I am burdened that we would see six visions: the vision of Christ, the vision of the church, the vision of the Body, the vision of the self, the vision of the world, and the vision of consecration.

PAUL'S SERVICE BEFORE HE GOT SAVED

With the history of the apostle Paul there are two parts, two sections: the part before he got saved and the part after he got saved. In both parts of his history he was a person serving God. Even before Paul was saved, he was a person dedicated to the service of God. If we read the New Testament carefully, we will realize that before he got saved Paul was a full-time worker, a full-time servant serving God.

However, there is a great difference between Paul's service before he got saved and his service after he got saved. First, before he got saved, Paul's service was a service without vision. Second, it is absolutely correct to say that his service was according to tradition and religion. Instead of serving with a vision, he was serving traditionally and religiously. Third, he was serving according to the knowledge of the Bible, that is, according to the letters, commandments, and regulations of the Old Testament. Fourth, he was serving in a condition of self-righteousness, serving in his self-righteousness. Fifth, he was serving with the full confidence that he was right. Sixth, his service was full of enthusiasm. He was serving not coolly but very enthusiastically, with his whole heart. Seventh, he had a goal and he served with a definite purpose. Thus, he was serving purposefully.

In principle, the work of nearly all of today's Christian workers is according to these seven points. In brief, these points are serving without a vision, serving traditionally and religiously, serving according to the knowledge of the Scripture in letters, serving in self-righteousness, serving with confidence, serving enthusiastically, and serving with a definite purpose. Are these things bad? They are not bad, but neither are they right. They may be good, but they are wrong.

BLESSED BLINDNESS

One day while Paul was serving God according to these seven points, he was on the way to Damascus. Suddenly, a heavenly vision came to him. This vision turned him, changed him, revolutionized him (Acts 9:1-5). This vision turned him from the old way of service. After he saw this vision, he became blind and very weak, even impotent. Before this vision came to him, Paul was clear, full of sight, and he was also potent, able to do many things. But suddenly a heavenly vision came to him, and Paul was changed. He became blind, unable to see anything, and impotent, unable to do anything. Before the vision came to him, he took the lead to do things, but after the vision came, he needed others to guide him.

At this juncture I would like to ask you a question: When was the time in your Christian life that you became blind and impotent? There needs to be a time in our Christian life when we realize that we are blind, when we realize that our sight is gone and that we do not know the direction but need others to lead us. It is a blessing to be blind in this way. Oh, blessed blindness! If you have never had a time in your Christian life when you became blind and impotent, then your service to God will be like Paul's service before he got saved. Those who serve in this way will be clear about everything and will have the full assurance that they are doing the right thing and that they know the right way to go on. But a blessed blindness comes upon those who are met by the heavenly vision. After this blindness comes upon us, there will be the inner anointing and the inner shining, the inner enlightening. The inner vision will increase more and more and will revolutionize the way we serve the Lord. In serving the Lord we will become a different person.

PAUL'S SERVICE AFTER HE GOT SAVED

Let us now contrast Paul's service after he got saved with his service before he got saved. In every aspect, his service now was opposite to the way he had served before.

Serving with a Vision

First, instead of serving without a vision, Paul served with a vision. He served with a vision not only in big things but even in small things. For example, in Galatians 2:1-2a he tells us about his going up to Jerusalem, the capital of the Jewish religion. "After a period of fourteen years I went up again to Jerusalem with Barnabas, taking Titus with me also. And I went up according to revelation." The fact that even such a move was done by revelation indicates that Paul was serving with a vision.

Serving Spiritually

Second, instead of serving traditionally and religiously, Paul now served spiritually. In Romans 1:9 he says, "God is my witness, whom I serve in my spirit in the gospel of His Son."

Can you discern what is traditional and religious from what is spiritual? Anything in the service of God that is not in the spirit but is according to the past is traditional and religious. We need to learn to serve not according to the past but in our spirit. This means that we should not imitate others and not even imitate our own past. If we imitate, our service will become religious and traditional. We need to have fresh contact with the Lord in spirit. However, if we serve merely according to what we know or according to what we remember, our serving will be traditional and religious. We need to exercise our spirit to contact the Lord to have something new and fresh. Then we will serve with our spirit, not with anything old.

Serving in Spirit

In contrast to serving according to the knowledge of the Bible in letters, after he got saved, Paul served in spirit. In Romans 2:29 Paul says, "He is a Jew who is one inwardly; and circumcision is of the heart, in spirit, not in letter." This indicates that we must serve not in letter but in spirit. Concerning this, 2 Corinthians 3:6 says that the ministers of the new covenant are ministers "not of the letter but of the Spirit; for the letter kills, but the Spirit gives life."

Serving with Christ

What is the opposite of serving with self-righteousness? The opposite of serving with self-righteousness is serving with Christ. When we do not have the heavenly vision, we have self-righteousness. When we have the heavenly vision, we no longer have self-righteousness—we have Christ. Then we serve with Christ, not with self-righteousness.

Serving in Faith

The opposite of serving with confidence is serving in faith or with faith. A person who serves God without having the vision is a person who serves in a natural way with much confidence. Those who are naturally strong in themselves do not need faith. Actually, a natural person cannot have faith; he has confidence instead of faith. But when we have the vision, we serve God not with confidence but with faith and in faith.

Serving Fervently

The opposite of serving enthusiastically is serving fervently. One who serves God fervently is not enthusiastic in himself but is fervent, inwardly burning in the Holy Spirit.

Serving by the Lord's Guidance

Now we need to ask, What is the opposite of serving God with a purpose? Instead of serving with a purpose, we should serve by the Lord's guidance. Whenever we do something with a purpose, we are behaving like a politician. Politicians always do things with a definite purpose. The more we act with a purpose, the more political we are. If we do not have the Lord's guidance to go to a particular place, yet we go to that place with a definite purpose, we are serving naturally and religiously.

Suppose you are going to the Far East. If you are going there with a definite purpose, you are going there as a politician. If you are asked why you are going to the Far East, you should be able to say, "My going to the Far East is of the Lord's guidance. I am not going there to accomplish a certain purpose. Rather, I am going to the Far East according to the Lord's guidance."

It is hard to discern guidance from purpose. You may say that when you have the guidance you have the purpose. Even if this is the situation, you need to act not according to the purpose but according to the guidance. In the book of Acts the apostles, the sent ones, went out, but it is difficult for us to see what their purpose was in going out. They went out by the Lord's guidance. They had no purpose, but they did have the Lord's guidance. Consider the example of Philip in Acts 8:26-39. The Holy Spirit guided him to contact the Ethiopian eunuch (v. 29). Philip did not have a purpose; he simply had the Lord's guidance. Before Philip contacted the eunuch, Philip had no idea concerning what would happen. His contacting the eunuch was not with a purpose; it was by the Lord's guidance.

OUR NEED FOR THE VISION

We need the vision, and we should pray much that we may have the vision. It is not adequate merely to learn how to serve. If we only learn certain things, what we learn will become something traditional and religious. It is good to learn something, but we need the vision to change what we have learned into something else.

I would ask you to pray that the Lord would grant you certain visions. First, we need the vision of Christ. We all need to see Christ, not merely have the knowledge about Christ. We also need the vision of the church, the vision of the Body, the vision of the self, and the vision of the world.

Regarding the self, we need a vision of the self so that the self may be exposed to us.

We may have much knowledge about Christ, the church, the Body, the self, and the world, but mere knowledge about these matters does not mean anything. For example, a sinful person may have a lot of knowledge about the gospel, yet he is still not saved. Only when what this sinner knows becomes a vision will he be saved. It is the vision, not the knowledge, that saves. A person may be told how sinful he is and how evil his heart is, and others may point out his shortcomings to him. But even then he is not convinced. He knows about these things, but he is not saved because as yet there is no vision. One day the vision comes to him, and under that vision he is saved.

The principle is the same with hearing about Christ, the church, the Body, the self, and the world. Only when we have the vision of Christ, the church, the Body, the self, and the world will we have the reality of what we have heard. Once we have reality we will have deliverance.

ASPECTS OF THE VISION OF CHRIST

Let us now go on to consider some aspects of the vision of Christ.

Christ Being the Center of God's Eternal Plan

We need the vision of Christ to see that He is the center of God's eternal plan. In addition, Christ is the center of all things belonging to God.

Christ Being the Embodiment of the Triune God

Christ is the very embodiment of the Triune God (Col. 2:9). We all know this, but to know is one thing and to have the vision of Christ as the embodiment of the Triune God is another thing.

Christ Having the First Place in Everything

Colossians 1:15-18 reveals that Christ must have the first place, the preeminence, in everything.

Christ Being the Essence of Our Daily Walk

We need to see clearly that Christ must be the essence, the substance, of our daily walk. This means that the essence of our daily walk is not humility or patience or love or kindness or good behavior. The essence of all these virtues must be Christ Himself. Our humility must be Christ. Our patience must be Christ. Our love must be Christ. Our kindness must be Christ. Our good behavior must be Christ. We need to see this vision.

If we see such a vision of Christ, we will never help others to have humility, patience, love, and kindness without Christ. We will never help them to be good without Christ. Rather, we will minister Christ to others. We will testify to others that Christ, the essence, the substance, of our daily walk, is humility, patience, love, kindness, and good behavior.

Christ Being the Reality of Our Service

Christ must also be the reality of our service, the reality of our ministry. No matter what kind of service we may do or what kind of ministry we may have, the reality of that service and ministry must be Christ. We should not minister knowledge and forms to others or impart gifts to others. Instead, we should minister Christ to others.

It is not easy to minister only Christ to others. Try to cease from ministering knowledge, forms, and gifts. If you do this, you may find that you have nothing to minister, for your ministry is full of knowledge, forms, and gifts. If you desert these things, you find that nothing remains. I would ask you to check your ministry in this way.

Christ's being the reality of our ministry and service includes His being the reality of the gospel. When we preach the gospel to sinners, we must have Christ as the reality of the gospel. This means that we should not merely preach the gospel but should preach the gospel with Christ. Christ is the gospel, and we should preach Him to others.

We need the vision of Christ as the reality of our ministry. We need the vision to see that our ministry must be full of Christ. If I come to contact a brother in order to have fellowship with him, I must not have only the knowledge of the Word but must have Christ as the reality of this fellowship. The knowledge of the Word is the means by which Christ is conveyed to this dear brother.

Knowledge, forms, and gifts should simply be the means to convey Christ to others. We may say that such things are the "wrappings" used in "packing" Christ as the content. Suppose you buy a diamond. The diamond is placed in a container, and then the container is wrapped. Neither the container nor the wrappings is the reality of the diamond which you have bought. The reality of the wrappings and the container is the diamond itself. If you take away the wrappings and the container, you will still have the diamond. However, with many so-called ministries today, once the "wrappings" and the "container" of teachings, forms, and gifts are removed, there is nothing left. There is no "diamond." Because this is the situation, I say once again that we need to have the vision of Christ as the reality of our ministry and service.

Christ Being the Expression of the Church Life

Christ must be the expression of the church life. The church life is for nothing other than Christ, and the church life should not express anything other than Christ. The church is not for knowledge, forms, gifts, and practices—the church is only for Christ. The church must be the expression of Christ.

Christ is the center of all things related to God. Christ is the embodiment of the Triune God. Christ must have the preeminence, the first place, in everything. Christ must be the essence, the substance, of our daily walk. Christ must be the reality of our ministry and service. Christ must be the expression of the church. We need to pray that we would see the vision of Christ in all these aspects.

THE DIFFERENCE BETWEEN VISION AND KNOWLEDGE

Some of us may have a question regarding the difference between vision and knowledge. A vision is something that catches us, whereas knowledge is something that we have to remember.

The first time I came to Los Angeles, in 1958, a friend brought me to an observatory on a hill in order to have a view of the city. I will never forget my impression of the city of Los Angeles as I looked down upon the city. I was caught by this view. But suppose my friend had merely given me some knowledge about Los Angeles and had told me about the streets and about how beautiful the city was at night. After a short time I would have forgotten what he had told me. However, I cannot forget the view of Los Angeles I had from that observatory on a hill. This is an illustration of the difference between seeing a vision and having knowledge.

THE BIBLE BECOMING TO US A BOOK OF CHRIST

We need to pray that the Lord would grant us the vision of Christ. All the knowledge about Christ that we have received needs to be transferred into the vision of Christ. We need to see that Christ is the center of God's eternal plan and of everything belonging to God and that Christ is the embodiment of the Triune God. We need to see that Christ must have the preeminence in all things, that Christ must be the essence of our daily walk, that Christ must be the reality of our ministry and service, and that Christ must be the only expression in the church life. Once we are caught by such a vision of Christ, we will lose sight of all other things. Then we will have only Christ, and we will no longer care to preach mere doctrines and knowledge.

When we have the vision of Christ, the Bible will become to us a book of Christ. Before we saw this vision, the Bible was to us not a book of Christ but a book of other things, in particular a book of doctrines and teachings. In reading the Bible we gained many things, but we did not gain Christ. But when we come to the Bible after we have seen the vision of Christ and have been caught by Christ and are occupied with Christ, in our reading of the Bible we will see Christ and we will care only for Christ.

People have told me that I speak too much concerning Christ and that I need to be balanced and speak about other things. To those who say this I would reply: "Brother, don't speak in this way. *You* need to be balanced, because you talk too much about things other than Christ. Perhaps I have only the diamond and display just the diamond, not the wrappings nor the container, but you have only the wrappings and the container. Don't tell me that I need the wrappings and the container— you need the diamond."

Because there are so many substitutes for Christ, we need to be recovered to Christ, even in an "extreme" way. We need the vision of Christ, and we need to cry out to the Lord, saying, "Lord, grant me the vision of Christ."

CHAPTER TWO

THE VISION OF THE CHURCH

Scripture Reading: Acts 8:1; 13:1; 1 Cor. 1:2; Rev. 1:11

We all need to see the vision of the church. The vision of the church is neglected more by Christians than the vision of Christ is. In a doctrinal way Christians may talk about Christ, but not even in a doctrinal way do they speak much concerning the church.

THE IMPORTANCE OF THE CHURCH— THE CHURCH BEING THE HEART'S DESIRE OF GOD

If we read the New Testament carefully, we will see the importance of the church. The New Testament reveals that without the church Christ would be isolated and unable to do anything. The New Testament especially reveals that the church is the heart's desire of God. God's desire in this age is to have the church.

We need to pray that we may see the importance of the church. The work of gospel preaching, the work of edifying the saints, and the work of teaching the Bible should all be for the church. Gospel preaching must not be for gospel preaching—it must be for the church. The edification of the saints must not be just for edification—it must be for the church. Teaching the Bible must not be simply for teaching the Bible—it must be for the church. In God's intention and according to His purpose, all such works are for the church. Even all the saved persons are for the church. We were saved not for ourselves and not merely for our salvation; we were saved for the building up of the church. The church is God's heart's desire.

We need to be impressed with the importance of the church and pray concerning this. Then we will no longer be indifferent about the matter of the church. We will see that what must come first is the church, not the preaching of the gospel, not the edification of the saints, and not the teaching of the Bible. The building up of the church should be our top priority.

THE PRACTICALITY OF THE CHURCH—
THE PRACTICE OF THE CHURCH
IN THIS DISPENSATION

We also need to see the practicality of the church. The church is very practical. We must have the church not in thought, in theory, or in teaching and not even in vision; we must have the church in practice. We all need to pray that we would see the practicality of the church.

The New Testament does not say much about the doctrine of the church, but it does give us a full picture of the practice of the church. Whereas some today have the doctrine of the church, the New Testament has the practice of the church. Therefore, in the New Testament we have the church not mostly and mainly in teaching but mostly and mainly in practice. In other words, in the New Testament we have the practicality of the church. We need to see the vision of the practicality of the church.

During the past century and a half, many Christian teachers have said that it is impossible for us to have the real church today. Some have said that the real church is invisible and that the visible church is not the real church. Furthermore, some Christian teachers claim that the real church is something for the future, not for the present. According to their understanding, since the real church is invisible and is something for the future, it is impossible for us to have a real church today. What we have today is just something visible, and according to these Christian teachers this is not the real church.

What kind of church do we have in the Bible? In the Bible are there two kinds of churches—the visible church and the invisible church? In the Bible do we have the church in the future and the church in the present?

According to the Bible we are now in the dispensation of the church, and the next dispensation will be the dispensation of the kingdom. If we do not have the church during the dispensation of the church, then in what dispensation will we have the church? Those who say that the church is something for the future need to realize that the next dispensation, the millennium, will be the dispensation not of the church but of the kingdom. After the dispensation of the kingdom there will be the new heaven and the new earth with the New Jerusalem. From this we can see that the teaching that the church is something for the future is absolutely unscriptural. The church must exist during the dispensation of the church, and the church must be practical. The book of Acts speaks of the church in Jerusalem (8:1) and the church in Antioch (13:1). This indicates that in the early days the church was visible and practical. Therefore, it is erroneous to say that the church is invisible.

THE LOCALITY OF THE CHURCH—
THE PRACTICAL EXPRESSION OF THE CHURCH

Next, we need to see that the practical expression of the church must be local. It must be in the place where we Christians are. This is extremely important. If we would have the practice of the church and therefore have the practicality of the church, we must have the local expression of the church. There is no other way. This means that we need to see the locality of the church.

Can you find a verse in the New Testament telling us that the church is in the heavens? There is no such verse. The New Testament speaks of the church in Jerusalem, the church in Antioch, the church in Corinth (1 Cor. 1:2), the church in Ephesus (Rev. 2:1), and the church in other cities (Rom. 16:1). All these churches may be called local churches. At the end of the New Testament, we have a picture of seven churches in seven cities (Rev. 1:4, 11; 2:1, 8, 12, 18; 3:1, 7, 14). In the New Testament it is very clear that the practical expression of the church must be local. We need to see this.

Because the situation today regarding the church is very complicated and confusing, we need to pray that we would see the church in a proper way according to the New Testament. We should avoid the complications and all the confusion and simply pay attention to what is revealed in the New Testament.

We may use driving a car as an illustration. If you drive on the highway, you will be clear about your direction. However, if you drive into the woods, you will not be clear but rather will be in a complicated situation. Concerning the church, some brothers who regard themselves as smart like to get into the "woods," into the complications. Eventually, they become very complicated and cannot get out of the "woods" of their complications. We need to learn to be simple and keep ourselves away from the complications. Simply read the New Testament, which speaks again and again about the locality of the church. Those who refuse to be simple in this matter but raise questions about the locality of the church end up in the "woods." Instead of raising questions and being complicated, we need to see a vision of the locality of the church.

THE UNIQUE ONENESS OF THE CHURCH—
THE PROPER GROUND OF THE CHURCH

We also need a vision of the unity of the church, a vision of the unique oneness of the church. When we speak here of the unity of the church, we speak of the unique unity, the only unity. In the Presbyterian denomination there may be a unity, and in the Methodist denomination there may also be a unity. But neither of these unities is the unique unity, the only unity. Rather, the unity of the Presbyterian denomination and the unity of the Methodist denomination are each a unity among many unities. What we need to see is the unique unity, not the unity among unities.

The unique unity, the unique oneness, of the church involves what we call the ground of the church. In ancient times the people of Israel had a unique unity in the good land of Canaan, with Jerusalem as its center. At that time the people of Israel were one. With them there was not more than one unity—there was the unique unity. The situation changed when the people of Israel were carried away into captivity. Most of them were carried away to Babylon, but some were carried away to Assyria and to Arabia. The people were scattered, and as a result they lost their unique unity.

Suppose some of those in Babylon had said, "As the people of God, we have to be one. Let us come together to practice unity." They would have had a unity, but it would have been not the unique unity but the unity in Babylon. Suppose those who had been carried away to Assyria and to Arabia had done the same thing. Then in addition to the unity in Babylon there would have been the unity in Assyria and the unity in Arabia. Each group would have had its own unity, but none of these unities would have been the genuine, unique unity. After seventy years some faithful ones, who stood with the Lord and took His word, went back to Jerusalem, and there they started to practice, to recover, the lost unity. The unity they practiced was the unique unity, the only unity. Thus, after the dispersion of the people of Israel and the return of the faithful ones, there were many unities, but only the unity in Jerusalem was the unique unity. The others were not the real unity; they were unities as divisions. Actually, those so-called unities were divisions. Only the unity in Jerusalem was the unique, the only, unity.

From this we see that there is only one ground for unity. If we have more than this one ground, the unity will be broken. The only ground for unity is the proper ground of unity. The proper ground of the unity of the church, therefore, is the ground of the unique unity. This is not the unity of the various denominations or groups; it is simply the unity of the church expressed in the places, the localities, where the saints are.

When we say that the church is expressed in the place where the saints are, we need to define what we mean by place. What is the limit of this place? The limit is not a house nor a street. In the New Testament there are no street churches or avenue churches. Today, however, so-called churches are designated by a street or an avenue. Some might say, "In the Bible there are no street churches, but there are house churches." Concerning house churches or home churches we need to be careful. Yes, the New Testament does mention the church in the house of certain saints (Rom. 16:5a; Col. 4:15-16). If we read the New Testament carefully, we will see that in these cases the church in the house was the same in limit as the church in the city. In other words, the limit of the house church was equal to the city. The church in that house was the church in that locality, in that city. Therefore, we cannot have a street church, nor an avenue church, nor a church on a college campus, nor a church in a house that is not also the church in the city. According to the New Testament we can have only a city church, that is, the church in the city where we are.

The reason for this limitation is that the church in the city, the local expression of the church, keeps the unity, the unique oneness, of the church. As long as we have the city church in Los Angeles, we are one. But if instead of the church in Los Angeles, we have street churches, or avenue churches, we will be divided. There will be a Westmoreland Avenue Church and an Elden Avenue Church. We would also be divided if we had churches in different houses, for there would be a church in the house of one brother and a different church in the house of another brother.

In God's wisdom and sovereignty the city keeps the unity, whereas streets and houses divide. If you go to San Francisco, you must go to the city church, the local church, the church in San Francisco. You should go not to a church on a street or in a house but to the church in the city. Likewise, you should go not to a church on a college campus but to the church in the city. To go to a so-called local church in a house is to get into division, but to go to a local church in a city is to get into unity.

We need a vision of this matter. Otherwise, we will have no way to go on with the church and eventually will have to drop the matter of the church. If we are not clear concerning the ground of the church, we will have no way to practice the church life. This has been the situation with a number of dear brothers. They talked a lot about the church, but eventually, because they would not take the ground of the church, they had no way to go on with the matter of the church and had to forsake this matter.

We should not despise the ground of the church or think that it is an insignificant matter. If we do not have the ground of the church, there is no way for us to have the proper practice of the church. Then we will have to give up the matter of the church. Some say, however, that if we take the church ground, we will have problems. But if we forsake the ground of the church, we will have even more problems and troubles. If we are to have the practice of the church, we must take a definite standing, and this standing must not be a wrong standing but the right standing—the standing on the ground of the church, the ground of unity. We need to come back to the original standing, the original ground, of the church.

We need to pray about the four matters we have covered concerning the vision of the church: the church being God's heart's desire, the practicality of the church, the locality of the church, and the definite local ground of unity. These four matters are a simple "map" for our "driving." If you are not clear about these matters, you will be lost as far as the church is concerned. No matter how much you talk about the church life and the Body life, you will be lost.

CAPTURED BY THE VISION OF THE CHURCH AND PAYING THE PRICE FOR IT

We need to be caught, captured, by these points concerning the vision of the church. By the Lord's mercy I can testify that since I was caught by this vision more than thirty years ago, I have never changed my tune. From the first day until now, my tune has been the same. But those who are not willing to take the way of the ground of the church often change their tune. For example, several years ago I was told by a particular group that they were the same as we are—a local expression of the church. In their writings they even used the words "local church." But now they oppose the matter of the church ground. Another example concerns a brother who, in response to our question of whether his meeting was on the ground of the church, said, "I cannot say that the meeting here is on the church ground, but we are working toward this goal." Now this person, who has been exposed as being two-faced, is absolutely opposed to the church ground. This is not the way for the children of God to conduct themselves. Our yes should be yes, and our no should be no.

Regarding the church, we need to have a clear vision, and then we must be ready to pay the price for it, even the price of our life. Then from the beginning to the end we will not change our tune. If we are willing to take the proper way concerning the church, our tune will always be the same. But those who are not willing to take this way will change their tune. They may talk about the church, but eventually they will give up the church and may even oppose it.

THE GROUND AND THE BUILDING

If we want to have a particular building, we must also have the lot on which the building stands, for the lot is the ground of the building. However, some may feel that the lot is earthly and has many problems and is too troublesome; therefore, they want the building without the lot. If you say that you like the building but will not take the lot, the ground, how can you have the building? In such a case, it would be impossible to have the building. This illustrates the attitude of some believers toward the ground of the church. They want to have the church, but they do not want to have the church ground. The result is that they do not have the church. Those who want a building without the lot cannot have the building. In like manner, those who want the church without the ground of the church cannot have the church.

ASKING THE LORD
FOR A CLEAR VISION OF THE CHURCH

We need to pray that we may see clearly the four matters that we have emphasized in this chapter. We need to see that the desire of God's heart is to have a church for His Christ. We need to see that the church is practical, that the church is not a matter in theory or merely in teaching. We also need to see that the church is local and that the church must have the proper ground. I would urge you to pray in a definite way about these four points. Otherwise, there will be no way for us to go on. Concerning these matters, you need to be simple. Do not be complicated, but in simplicity ask the Lord to show you a clear vision of these four points.

CHAPTER THREE

THE VISION OF THE BODY

Scripture Reading: Rom. 12:1-2; 1 Cor. 12:12-27; Eph. 4:16

Prayer: Lord, how we thank You for this precious hour that we may come to learn the way of Your recovery. O Lord, You know that our heart is full of gratitude for Your mercy and grace. We bow before You to confess that we are still sinful, that we are still in the old nature, and that we are still so much in the self. How much we still have self-seeking, self-interest, self-righteousness, and self-consciousness. Lord, how much we need Your cleansing! Lord, we have no merit, no good, for us to stand on. But, Lord, we have Your blood as our covering and as our standing. Lord, grant us a living word to speak something about Your mystery, the Body of Christ. Lord, grant us the inner grace that we need for this matter. How much we need You as the inner grace! O Lord, draw us to love You. Lord, draw us to go with You that we may be one with You and may be built up as Your living Body. Lord, deliver us from so many distracting elements and frustrating things and deliver us from our self that we may be truly one in Spirit. Lord, You know that we are weak. We look to You for Your help. In Your precious name.

In this chapter we come to the third vision, the vision of the Body. Before we consider this vision, however, let us review what we have covered regarding the vision of Christ and the vision of the church.

CHANGED FROM TRADITION TO VISION

We have seen that the real service, work, and ministry that we could render to the Lord must be something of the heavenly vision, not something traditional, religious, or natural. In the first chapter we pointed out that in the first part of his life, Paul's service was according to tradition and religion and was without vision. He had the confidence that he was serving God, but he was serving according to the letter, knowledge, teaching, and regulations of the Old Testament. But after he received the heavenly vision, his service, work, and ministry were changed from tradition to vision. He served no longer according to the traditions of his forefathers or according to knowledge and regulations but according to the heavenly vision, the present vision. In Galatians 2 Paul went up to Jerusalem not by regulation but by revelation, by vision. He had come to see something, so he went up to Jerusalem. As we read his Epistles we can see that Paul was a man full of visions.

CAUGHT BY THE VISION OF CHRIST

The first of these visions is the vision of Christ. To have the vision of Christ is to see that Christ is the embodiment of the Triune God and the center of all things related to God. Christ is the center of God's plan, of God's eternal intention. Christ is also the center of God's work, God's creation, and God's redemption. Christ is the center of all that God has planned to do. Christ must have the preeminence in everything; He must have the first place in all things. We need to apply this Christ to our life, ministry, and church life. Christ must be the essence, the substance, of our Christian walk and the reality of our work, service, and ministry. Our ministry should be a ministry of Christ, full of Christ. Furthermore, Christ must be the content and expression of the church life. The church should be an expression of nothing other than the all-inclusive Christ. We all need such a vision of Christ.

In order to see the vision of Christ, you may need to pray earnestly for a period of time. You may need to cry out to the Lord day by day, saying, "Lord, reveal Yourself to me that I may see. Lord, I do not just need to know—I need to see. I need to be impressed by the vision concerning Yourself." Eventually something like a veil will be opened to you, and within you there will be an inner revelation, an inner unveiling. Then, as was the case with Paul, "something like scales" (Acts 9:18) will fall from your eyes, and you will be able to say, "Before now I knew something about Christ, but I did not have the vision. Now I see!" Once you were veiled, but the veil has been lifted and the curtain has been opened. No human word can explain this; it is something that you must experience.

You may hear messages about Christ as the embodiment of the Triune God, as the center of the things of God, as the One who has the first place in everything, as the essence of our Christian life, as the reality of our service, and as the content and expression of the church life. You may hear about all these matters, but one day the veil will be opened and you will see the vision of Christ. Once you see this vision you will be caught by it. From that time onward your burden will be to minister Christ to others. If you speak about something other than Christ, you will not have the inner anointing. But the more you speak concerning Christ, the more you will have the inner anointing. You are now "shut in" with Christ, kept away from mere knowledge, for your eyes have been opened and you have seen the vision of Christ.

GOD'S DESIRE TO HAVE THE CHURCH

If you would be a proper Christian, you need to see not only the vision of Christ but also the vision of the church. You need to see that God's desire is to have the church. The Holy Spirit will point out to you that God's purpose in creating the universe was to produce the church. Redemption also is for the church. All that God does is for the church, and every kind of work and ministry should be for the church. Gospel preaching is for the church. Edifying the saints is for the church. Teaching the Bible is for the church. We have been saved for the church, not for ourselves nor for any other purpose. The desire of God's heart is to have the church, and we were saved to be built up as the church. We must have this vision.

I believe that if you really mean business with the Lord and take sides with Him, sooner or later He will open your eyes to see that His desire in this universe is to have the

church. All other things are secondary. The primary thing is
that the church is God's heart's desire.

Seeing this will not only rescue you from the wrong
concept and understanding; it will revolutionize your Christian service. You will see that God's intention is to have the
church, not just to have the gospel preached that others may
be brought to the Lord, nor just to have others helped to seek
the Lord, love the Lord, and be spiritual. Everything you do
in your work and service for the Lord will be for the building
up of the church. Whatever you are and whatever you do will
be for the church.

Consider the ministry of the apostle Paul. What did Paul
do after he had been changed, revolutionized, to this way of
vision? Everything he did was for the church. Strictly
speaking, he did not have what we may call "a piece of work."
He simply did everything for the church. Apart from the
church, Paul did not have anything. Whatever he was and
whatever he did were for the church. If the church had been
taken away, Paul would have had nothing left.

I would ask you to check yourself by comparing yourself
with Paul. I am concerned that you have many things besides
the church. You may have some good works, but these good
works are besides the church. This proves that you are wrong.
The church is the real test that proves what we are and where
we are. The church is God's desire.

THE PRACTICALITY OF THE CHURCH TODAY

We need to see that the church is not something "in the
air" but is very real and practical. In the New Testament we
do not have much teaching about the church, but we surely
have the practicality of the church. In the New Testament
the church was a matter that was put into practice. Therefore,
we today must have the practice of the church.

We should not say that the church is invisible or that it
is something for the future. The church is certainly visible.
In the New Testament we do not read about an invisible
church nor about a church in the future. In the future there
will be not the dispensation of the church but the dispensation
of the kingdom. Do not postpone the church. The church must

be today. If you do not have the church on the earth in this life, then where and when will you have the church? After you die will you go to a place where you will have the church life? If the church life is postponed until the future, where will this future church life be? Can you show me a verse or a passage of Scripture which tells us that after we die we will go to heaven and there have good church meetings with Paul and Peter? Can you show me where the Bible tells us that we will have the proper church life, the so-called invisible yet real church life, in the future in heaven? There is not such a verse. Neither is there a verse which tells us that the church will be in the future.

Why do people take in the thought that the church on earth today is not the real church, that the real church is the so-called invisible church? Why do people accept the teaching that the church is something for the future? The church must be practical today. We all need to see the vision of the practicality of the church.

BEING TROUBLEMAKERS
TO ESTABLISH LOCAL CHURCHES

The church is also local. Since the church must be local, wherever you are is the right place for you to have the church. The church should be in the very place where you are. A place may seem to be good, but if that place is without a church, it is a hell. On the contrary, any place with a church is a heaven.

This reminds us of Jacob's experience in Genesis 28. "He dreamed, and behold a ladder set up on the earth, and the top of it reached to heaven: and behold the angels of God ascending and descending on it" (v. 12). When Jacob awoke he said, "How dreadful is this place! this is none other but the house of God, and this is the gate of heaven" (v. 17). Then he called the name of that place "Bethel," which means "the house of God." Today Bethel, the house of God, is the church (1 Tim. 3:15). Wherever there is the church, the house of God, that place is the gate of heaven. The only place that is good for us today is a place where there is the church.

Wherever we go and wherever we are, there must be a church. Concerning this matter of the church, we should be troublemakers. We should trouble others for the producing of the church. If there is not a church in a particular locality, we should not let the people there be at peace. Rather, we should cause trouble so that there may be a church in that locality. We should declare to the universe, "If there is no church in this place, I do not have a dwelling place. I must have a home, and for this I must cause trouble."

I expect that the day will come when we all, like Paul, will be troublemakers. We need to trouble the entire country for the sake of producing the church. Wherever Paul and the other apostles went, there was trouble. Before they came to a particular place, the people were at peace. But after these troublemakers arrived, the whole city was troubled, disturbed. Acts 17:6 says, "These men who have upset the world have come here also." It is by upsetting the world, by causing trouble, that we establish and build up the church.

SETTLED ON THE GROUND OF THE UNIQUE UNITY

We also need to see that the church has its definite ground—the ground of the unique unity. This is the ground not merely of unity but of the unique unity. Today there are many different kinds of unities. Only one unity is the unique unity; all other unities are divisions. We need to have a clear vision concerning this.

I can say with full assurance that only when you are settled with this unique ground of unity will your Christian life be settled. If you are not settled regarding the ground, you will be continually wandering and changing your tune. Today you have one tune, but tomorrow your tune will change. You will not be settled and your tune will not be constant until you are settled with and on the ground of the unique unity.

You need to see that the church is the desire of God's heart, and you need to see that the church is practical and local. Then you need to see that among so many divisions and in the midst of so much confusion, there is the definite standing of the church, and this standing is the ground of the unique unity. If you see these things, you will not care about how many others will come to this ground. You will realize that, as far as you are concerned, as long as you are on this ground, you are settled. You are like the Israelites who came back to Jerusalem and who became settled there. We need to see such a vision of the church that we become settled on the ground of the unique unity.

THE DIFFERENCE BETWEEN THE VISION OF THE CHURCH AND THE VISION OF THE BODY

After we have seen the vision of Christ and the vision of the church, we need to see the vision of the Body. You may be wondering what the difference is between the vision of the church and the vision of the Body. By the Lord's mercy many of us have been brought to the ground of the church and are now practicing the church life on the proper ground. Although we have been brought to a realization of the ground of the unique unity, we still need the realization of the Body. We need to see the vision that we are members of the Body and that we need to be built up together and related to one another. It is not sufficient just to be brought to a realization concerning the church ground, but on this definite ground we need to be built up as the Body. The three main portions of the New Testament which speak of the Body are Romans 12, 1 Corinthians 12, and Ephesians 4.

THREE HINDRANCES

First, we need to see the vision of Christ; second, the vision of the church; and third, the vision of the Body. With respect to each of these visions, there is a particular hindrance.

The Substitutes of Christ

Formerly you did not see the vision of Christ, but now you see this vision. What kept you from seeing the vision of Christ before now? What hindered you, and what hinders others today, from seeing the vision of Christ? The answer is that people are hindered from seeing Christ by the various substitutes. Many things are substitutions for Christ, and these are the hindrance to seeing the vision of Christ.

The Unwillingness to Pay the Price

Some may say that divisions are what hinder them from seeing the vision of the church. To speak like this is to speak in a doctrinal way. I prefer to talk about this matter in an experiential way. People oppose the church, especially the ground of the church, because of the cost involved in coming to the church ground. Some claim that they cannot understand this matter of the ground of the church. Actually, they do understand it, but they are unwilling to pay the price to meet on the church ground. They may offer an excuse, saying, "I do not like to be so narrow. I love all the children of God, and I want to be broad-minded. I cannot understand this strange speaking about the ground of the church." This sounds good, but it is actually a cloak that covers the unwillingness to pay the price. People talk like this because of the cost involved. The Lord knows and their conscience knows that they are not faithful to the Lord in the matter of the cost of practicing the church life on the proper ground.

We should not argue with such people. When people came to argue with Brother Nee, he would smile and say, "You can argue with me, but there is something within you that agrees with me." Today, people may argue with us about the ground of the church, but something within them takes sides with us regarding this. Their conscience knows that they are hindered by the cost, by the price. For more than thirty years we have seen people come and go. In each case they were frustrated by the cost.

The Self

Whereas the substitutes are the hindrance to seeing the vision of Christ and the cost is the hindrance to seeing the vision of the church, the hindrance to seeing the vision of the Body and to practicing the Body life is the self. Yes, we are practicing the church life on the proper ground of the church, but are we built up together? Are we rightly related to one another? Are we fitly framed together? We meet together, but we may not be built up together. We have the meeting, but we do not have the building. We need a vision of the Body, but this vision is at the cost of the self. If we are to be built up in the Body, the self must go. This is why we also need to see (in the next chapter) the vision of the self. The self is a problem to the Body.

THE SUBTLETY OF THE ENEMY
IN OPPOSING THE CHURCH

Once we see the vision of Christ, we are qualified to see the vision of the church. However, with the matter of the church, you may sense that there is a cost and that you will have to pay the price. If you are not willing to pay the price, you may go back to the vision of Christ and say, "It is sufficient that we know Christ. Christ is everything. We should not talk about the church. Let us speak to others concerning Christ, telling them what He is. Let us preach Christ to sinners and let us minister Christ to the saints. It is enough that we talk about Christ. There is no need for us to talk about the church." This kind of speaking is subtle; it is a sugar-coated excuse for not paying the price to practice the church life on the ground of the unique unity.

At this juncture let us consider the Lord's word to Peter in Matthew 16. Immediately after Peter declared concerning the Lord Jesus, "You are the Christ, the Son of the living God," He said to him, "Upon this rock I will build My church" (vv. 16, 18). This indicates that knowing Christ and experiencing Christ are for the church. Today some condemn us, saying that we are too much for the church, that we make the church greater than Christ. Some go so far as to say that we make the church an idol. This argument is subtle. Oh, the subtlety of the enemy! Christ died on the cross for the church (Eph. 5:25). If we are too much for the church, Christ was the first one to be too much.

LOSING THE SELF FOR THE BUILDING UP OF THE BODY

After we have seen the vision of the church, the Lord will open our eyes to see the Body. We will see that we need to be built up in the Body. We are not just members of the church; we are members of the Body. For the Body we must not only pay a price—we must lose the self.

By the Lord's mercy I can testify that from the time I first began to meet on the proper ground more than thirty years ago, I have not changed in this matter. Furthermore, after coming to this ground, by the Lord's mercy I began to realize and practice the Body, and I am still practicing the Body today. I have not moved from this ground, and I have not changed my position on this ground.

You may not change in the matter of the ground, but you may change your position on the ground. As an illustration let us suppose that various kinds of material are brought to a certain lot, or site, as the ground. All these materials are now on the same ground. However, it is possible for them to remain on the building site and yet have a change of position on that site. In like manner, we have been brought to the proper ground of the church and on this ground we are practicing the church life. Perhaps a "soft" brother is put together with a "hard" brother. The "soft" one may cry out to the Lord, saying, "Lord, I cannot stand being with this brother. I want to have a change." This brother is seeking a change not of the ground but a change of position on the ground. He remains on the ground, but he wants a change of relationship on the ground. This is the situation with many in the church life, and it may be your situation. You have not changed concerning the ground, but you may have changed in position, in relationship, again and again.

Some of today's Christians are wandering among the denominations, among different grounds. At present they are meeting with a particular group, but tomorrow they may begin to meet with a different group. Others are not wandering among different grounds, but they are wandering in their position on the proper ground. This indicates that with them there is a lack of building. They have not been built up with others. But once we have been built up, just as the materials in a house or a meeting hall cannot change their position, so we will not be able to change our position. We are fixed in place and can no longer wander from one position to another.

Why is it so difficult for us to be built up? The difficulty is the self. It does not matter whether the self is good or bad, pleasant or ugly. As long as there is the self, there cannot be any building.

For instance, some brothers have a dominating self, and because of this dominating self they cannot go along with others in doing things for the church. No matter what the situation may be, these brothers must be the dominating ones. How, then, can they have the building? In order for them to be built up with others, the self must be broken. The problem is not their strong character; it is their dominating self. It may be right for them to be strong, but they should not dominate others. A person who is built up with others may be very strong, but he is properly related to others and constantly has fellowship with others. A marble column in a building is strong, but it is related to others. It is strong, but it does not dominate. The situation is the same with a strong brother who has been built up with others in the Body.

BROKEN UNDER THE VISION OF THE BODY

We need to learn the lessons regarding the self so that we may be built up in the Body. As we are considering this matter of the self, I would urge you to receive more grace so that the self might be exposed. In being built up with others, the greatest problem is the self. Some brothers and sisters like others to praise them or to say something good about them. If you were to speak to them frankly and truthfully in love, they would be hurt and offended because they are so much in the self. This indicates that even though such brothers and sisters are meeting on the ground of the church, it is very hard for them to be built up because of the self.

You need to see the vision of the Body. This vision will break you. You will be broken under the vision of the Body. You will realize that the only way for you to be built up in the Body is for you to be broken. The only way to realize the Body is to be broken.

BUILT, SATISFIED, AND WRECKED

After you see the vision of the Body, you will be not only settled but also built. Only then will you be satisfied in your Christian life. Until you are built up in the Body, you cannot

be satisfied. No matter what you say, the inner feeling will
tell you that you are not satisfied. But one day you will be
built up, and then you will be able to say, "Lord, praise You
that I am here. I am built and now I am satisfied. Because
I am built I am finished. I am not good for anything else. I
have been wrecked by this building."

Many brothers are afraid to be built because they realize
that once they are built, they will be finished, "wrecked."
They desire to preserve themselves as "good material." They
know that once they are built, they will be "wrecked," good
for nothing except the building. I agree that to be built means
that we are no longer good for anything else. Consider the
lintel of a door. The material used in making the lintel has
been "wrecked," for now it is good only for that lintel.
Likewise, when we are built, we are finished. We are no
longer a piece of "good material"; we are part of the building.
This is what the Lord needs today.

There must come a time when you will be able to say,
"Lord, I am satisfied here in the building, but I am also
wrecked. I have been wrecked by You, and I am good only to
be part of the building." Because you have been "wrecked,"
finished, you will no longer be welcomed by others or praised
by others. You will no longer be useful to others, and they
will forget you. But although you will be forgotten by others,
you will be remembered by the Lord. He remembers you
because you are in the building.

I can testify that, by the Lord's mercy, I have never
changed my ground, I have never changed my position, and
I have never changed my co-workers. Because I have been
built, I am finished and do not expect anything better. The
vision of the Body has kept me from changing my tune. This
is not something of me; it is of the Lord's mercy.

OUR NEED TO BE BUILT UP TOGETHER

Have you ever seen the building among today's Christians?
There are all kinds of Christian meetings and Christian
groups, but there is no building. I believe that in these last
days the Lord's goal is the building up of the Body. It is not
adequate that we realize that Christ is everything and then

come together to practice the proper church life. We need to be built up together as members of the Body. Unless you are built up with others, you will not be stable with the matter of the church ground. Let us suppose as an illustration that some building materials are placed on a particular lot or building site. If these materials are simply left there lying on the ground, someone could come and take them away. However, if these materials are built up together, they will be stable in their position on the site. They cannot leave the site unless the entire building is torn down. In like manner, our position on the ground of the church will not be stable until we are built into the building, into the Body.

SEEING THE VISION OF THE BODY
AND RENOUNCING THE SELF
FOR THE BUILDING UP OF THE BODY

We need to realize that the hindrance to the building up of the Body is the self. Certain brothers and sisters have seen something of Christ and of the church and have come to the ground of the church. However, they have never opened themselves to others. Outwardly they do not criticize the elders and they seem to be very nice, but inwardly they are critical. The problem with them is not sin—it is the self. This indicates that in order to be built up, we need to be opened, exposed, and broken. We should be able to present ourselves to others in fellowship and tell them that we are ready for whatever is necessary to be built up with them.

I believe that in this country the Lord intends to build up a real expression of the Body. His desire is not that we simply come together and meet together but that we be built up together.

Oh, how we need the vision of the Body! We need to be burdened to pray, "Lord, help me to see the vision of the Body. It is not good enough just to be a Christian and a member of the church. I must be built up in the Body. In a practical way, I must be a member of the living Body. I must have fellowship with others and be related to others in the Body."

God's intention is to have the church, and this church must

be the Body. We must be built up in the Body, but the hindrance to this building is the self, one of the last things in us to be dealt with by the Lord. If we would be built up in the Body, the self must be condemned, denied, rejected, and renounced. Day by day the self must be renounced in all things. Only when the self is renounced will we have the Body and be genuine members of the Body.

It is by the Body that God's purpose will be fulfilled; it is by the Body that Christ will be expressed; and it is by the Body that the enemy of God will be defeated. Nothing is as worthy as the Body. Not even the preaching of the gospel is as worthy as the Body. Nothing can compare with the building up of the Body. May we all see the vision of the Body and be captured by this vision.

CHAPTER FOUR

THE VISION OF THE SELF

Scripture Reading: Matt. 16:21-26; Luke 9:23-25; Gen. 3:1-6

If we would see the vision of the self, we need to pay careful attention to Matthew 16:21-26, Luke 9:23-25, and Genesis 3:1-6.

SATAN, THE MIND, THE SELF, AND THE NATURAL LIFE

Matthew 16:21 tells us that Jesus "began to show to His disciples that He must go to Jerusalem and suffer many things from the elders and chief priests and scribes and be killed and on the third day be raised." When Peter heard this, he "took Him aside and began to rebuke Him, saying, God be merciful to You, Lord! This shall by no means happen to You!" (v. 22). Jesus turned and said to Peter, "Get behind Me, Satan! You are a stumbling block to Me, for you are not setting your mind on the things of God, but on the things of men" (v. 23). Then Jesus said to His disciples, "If anyone wants to come after Me, let him deny himself and take up his cross and follow Me. For whoever wants to save his soul-life shall lose it; but whoever loses his soul-life for My sake shall find it. For what shall a man be profited if he gains the whole world, but forfeits his soul-life? Or what shall a man give in exchange for his soul-life?" (vv. 24-26). The Greek word translated "soul-life" here is *psuche,* the word for "soul." Whenever the New Testament speaks of the divine life, eternal life, the life of God, it uses the word *zoe,* but when it speaks of the soulish life, the soul-life, it uses the word *psuche.*

In these verses there are four things which are closely related to one another: Satan, the mind, the self, and the natural life. In verse 23a Jesus said to Peter, "Get behind

Me, Satan!" Then He went on to speak about the mind: "You
are not setting your mind on the things of God, but on the
things of men" (v. 23b). Following this, we have the self in
verse 24 and the natural life, here called the soul-life, in
verses 25 and 26. The soul-life, or the natural life, is the self;
the self is in the mind; and the mind is occupied by Satan.

SELF—THE EMBODIMENT OF SATAN

As we consider these matters, we eventually realize what
the self is. The self is the embodiment of Satan. As Christ
is the embodiment of God, so the self is the embodiment of
Satan. This is indicated by the fact that the Lord Jesus said
to Peter, "Get behind Me, Satan!" The Lord was speaking to
Peter, yet He called Peter Satan because Satan was embodied
in Peter. Where was Satan embodied? Satan was embodied in
Peter's soul by occupying his mind. The mind is the leading
part of the soul and the representative of the soul. To take
over a person's mind is to take over the entire person.

We need to be impressed with these four matters: Satan,
the mind, the self, and the natural life. The soul is the natural
life. The natural life is the self. The self is in the mind, which
is occupied by Satan. The self is thus the embodiment of
Satan.

At this point it would be helpful to compare Luke 9:25 to
Matthew 16:26. In Luke 9:25 the Lord Jesus says, "What is
a man profited if he gains the whole world but loses or forfeits
himself?" As we have seen, in Matthew 16:26 the Lord Jesus
speaks of losing the soul-life. Whereas Matthew 16:26 speaks
of "soul-life," in Luke 9:25 "soul-life" is replaced by "himself."
This indicates that our soul-life is our self. These are
synonyms. The self is the soul-life and the soul-life is the
self.

THE ORIGIN OF THE SELF

What is the origin of the self? Since God did not create
the self, where did the self come from? In order to answer
the question concerning the origin of the self, it would be
helpful to consider the difference between the body and the
flesh.

God created for man a body that was good, pure, and sinless. The flesh is also the body, but it is the corrupted, ruined body. Satan injected sin into the human body created by God, and in this way the body was corrupted and ruined, becoming the flesh. The flesh, therefore, is the body corrupted by sin. We may also say that the flesh is the body plus sin. The sin which is in man's body is the very nature of Satan. In Romans 6 and 7 sin is personified, for it is likened to a living person that dwells in us (7:17, 20), works in us (v. 8), deceives us (v. 11), kills us (v. 11), and reigns in us (6:12, 14). This sin which, like a living person, can force us to do things against our will, is the nature of Satan. We may even say that sin is Satan. Because sin has been injected into our body and is now in the members of our body, our body has been corrupted and has become the flesh.

The situation is similar with the self. The body became the flesh because something of Satan—sin—was injected into it. How did the soul become the self? The soul became the self when something of Satan was added to the soul. The thing that was added to the soul was the thought, or the mind, of Satan. Therefore, the self is the soul plus the satanic mind, the mind of Satan. When the mind, the thought, of Satan was injected into the human soul, the human soul was corrupted and became the self.

The body has been changed into the flesh, and the soul has been changed into the self. Which of these changes took place first? The answer to this question is found in Genesis 3:1-6. Here we see that before Eve took the fruit of the tree of the knowledge of good and evil into her body, the thought, the mind, of Satan was injected into her soul. Satan came to Eve with the intention of putting his thought into her mind. Satan did this when he said to her, "Yea, hath God said, Ye shall not eat of every tree of the garden?" (v. 1). This was an appeal to Eve's mind. Eve answered Satan (vv. 2-3), but as soon as she did so, she was "hooked" in her mind by the "bait" of Satan's thought.

Day after day Satan tries to do the same thing with us, sending some sweet, enticing bait to our mind. For instance, in the morning, as you are waking up, a critical thought concerning the church in Los Angeles may suddenly enter your mind. Such a thought is Satan's bait, and the more you pay attention to this bait, the more you will be hooked by Satan. Eventually, you may decide to give up the church life. Satan did not come to Eve to fight with her or to speak against her. Rather, he came in a nice way to "help" her. In response to Satan's question, she said, "We may eat of the fruit of the trees of the garden: but of the fruit of the tree which is in the midst of the garden, God hath said, Ye shall not eat of it, neither shall ye touch it, lest ye die" (vv. 2-3). At this point Eve was already caught by Satan who, taking Eve's word as his basis, said to her, "Ye shall not surely die: for God doth know that in the day ye eat thereof, then your eyes shall be opened, and ye shall be as gods, knowing good and evil" (vv. 4-5). Satan seemed to be saying to the woman, "I am here as your good friend to tell you a secret. God is fooling you. If you eat of the fruit of this tree, you will be like a god."

Through this satanic assault, Eve's mind was attacked. Then her mind was poisoned by the satanic thought which had been injected into her. After this, her emotion was aroused when she "saw that the tree was good for food, and that it was pleasant to the eyes, and a tree to be desired to make one wise" (v. 6a). Next, her will was exercised to make a decision to eat of the fruit of the tree of the knowledge of good and evil. "She took of the fruit thereof, and did eat" (v. 6b). By this time every part of the soul—the mind, the emotion, and the will—had been poisoned.

SIN, THE SELF, AND THE WORLD

Two great problems are sin in the body and self in the soul. In addition, as we will see in the next chapter, there is the problem of the world outside of us. These three things— sin, the self, and the world—are three strands of a strong cord that binds us. No one can release himself from this binding cord, a cord that is a composition of sin, the self, and the world.

Christians may be quite clear about sin, but not many are clear about the self and the world. In their experience one of the three strands—sin—has been broken, but the other two strands—the self and the world—have not been broken. As a result they are still under the bondage of the self on the inside and of the world on the outside. In this chapter we need to see that the strand of the self must be cut. In the next chapter we will see that the strand of the world must also be cut. Only when all three strands of this binding cord have been cut will we be released from bondage.

THE SELF BEING THE SOUL WHICH IS DECLARING INDEPENDENCE FROM GOD

We have seen that the origin of the self was Satan's injecting his thought into the human mind. Now we need to see that the self is the soul being independent of God. Whenever the soul is not dependent on God but is independent of Him, the soul immediately becomes the self. This means that whenever we do something by ourselves without depending on God we are in the self. No matter what we are and no matter what we do, as long as we are independent of God we are in the self.

God created man as a soul to be always dependent on Him. Man is a soul (Gen. 2:7), and as a soul he should depend on God for everything. We may use married life as an illustration of the dependence of the soul on God. A wife should depend on her husband. This is indicated by a bride's wearing a head covering on her wedding day. Her wearing a head covering signifies that she will take her husband as her head and will depend on him. Otherwise, there will be two heads, and this will lead to contradicting, fighting, and even divorce. Just as a wife should depend on her husband, so the soul should depend on God.

However, the soul has become the self. The self is simply the soul declaring independence from God. If we have the vision of the self, we will see what the self is—the soul declaring its independence from God. If we see this vision, we will realize that we can no longer be independent of God. Then we will say, "I must depend on God all the time. Whatever I do, I must depend on God. Whatever I am, I must depend on God."

THE SELF BEING THE GREATEST PROBLEM
TO THE BUILDING UP OF THE BODY

Because the self is something independent, the self is the greatest problem to the building up of the Body. We should be dependent not only on God but also on the Body, on the brothers and sisters. Whenever we are independent of the brothers and sisters, we are in the self, in the independent soul. For us today, being independent of the Body is equal to being independent of God. This is a matter not of doctrine but of experience. If you check with your experience, you will realize that when you were independent of the brothers and sisters, you had the sense that you were also independent of God. Likewise, when you were isolated from the brothers and sisters, you had the sense that you were also isolated from God.

When some hear this, they may say, "Isn't the Lord omnipresent? Since the Lord is everywhere, I can have His presence anywhere. I can have the Lord's presence in my home or in any other place." However, having the Lord's presence depends on whether or not you are dependent on the Body and are rightly related to the Body. If you are rightly related to the Body, you will have the Lord's presence in every place. But if you are not rightly related to the Body, then no matter where you may be, you will not have the Lord's presence. Therefore, having the Lord's presence depends on our relationship with the Body. If we are wrong with the Body, we will not sense that we have the Lord's presence. If we are right with the Body, wherever we may go we will have the sense of His presence.

In order to be dependent on the Lord, we must be dependent on the Body. If we are dependent on the Body, then we will also be dependent on the Lord. You may wonder why you do not have a deep sense of the Lord's presence. You do not have the Lord's presence, because you are isolated from the Body, because you are not properly related to the members of the Body. Endeavor to be built up and to be right with the Body. If you are right with the Body and are built up in the Body, you will surely sense the Lord's presence.

THE LORD HAVING REGARD NOT FOR WHAT WE DO
BUT FOR OUR DEPENDENCE ON HIM

We have seen that the self is the independent soul. In doing things, our motive, intention, aim, and goal may all be right, but if we are independent, we are in the self. This may be our situation even in preaching the gospel, for we may preach the gospel in the self and by the self. We may also do certain other works for the Lord, but we may do them in the self and by the self.

I am very grateful to the Lord for Matthew 16:21-26. Here Peter was not doing something evil to the Lord. On the contrary, he was acting out of love for Him and intended to do something good for Him. Nevertheless, because Peter was independent of the Lord, the Lord turned to Peter and said, "Get behind Me, Satan!" This indicates that no matter what we do, even if it is something very good, we are in the self whenever we are independent of the Lord.

From this we see that the Lord Jesus does not have regard for what we do; rather, He has regard for our dependence on Him. If we see this, we will pay attention not to what we do but to whether or not we are dependent on the Lord. We need to ask ourselves: Am I independent of the Lord or am I dependent on Him? If we are independent of the Lord, we are in the self. If we are dependent on the Lord, we are spontaneously dependent on the Body.

SEEING THE VISION OF THE SELF
AND HATING OUR INDEPENDENCE
FROM THE LORD AND THE BODY

The Lord and the Body are one. If you are dependent on the Lord, you are dependent on the Body. If you are dependent on the Body, you are dependent on the Lord. If you are independent of the Body, you are spontaneously independent of the Lord and are in the self, no matter how many good things you intend to do. Furthermore, because you are in the self, you are incorporated with Satan. In this corporation the self is the general manager and Satan is the president.

Oh, how we need to see the vision of the self! If we see this vision, we will hate our independence from the Lord and the Body. Then we will love the dependence on the Body, on the brothers and sisters, and on the Lord. As long as we have no dependence on the Lord and on the Body, the self is here. But when we have dependence, the self is gone.

DEPENDENCE BRINGING GENUINE PEACE

Dependence brings peace. Actually, dependence is the real peace. How do we know that we are dependent on God? We know it by the genuine peace within us. When we are dependent on God, we are full of peace.

Some brothers who are independent of the Body may claim that they are doing something for God. However, they do not have peace within them. The more they claim that they are doing something for God, the more they have the sense that they are not at peace. But if you ask them if they have peace, they will say that they have peace. They may argue, saying, "I have peace. What need is there for me to be related to you people? I am preaching the gospel and doing the work of the Lord, and I have peace." What kind of peace is this? It is not the genuine peace; it is a self-made peace, a peace that is made and maintained by the self.

When we are dependent on the Lord and on the Body, there is no need for the self to manufacture a kind of peace and then strive to maintain this peace. A man-made peace is a peace which needs the self to sustain it. As soon as the self stops working at sustaining this kind of peace, the peace disappears. Genuine peace does not need to be sustained by the self. If you have a real dependence on the Lord and on the Body, automatically the peace will be there. You will know and others also will know that you are truly at peace.

Those who are independent of the Body not only do not have genuine peace within but also are exercised to talk with others in order to get the confirmation which they are seeking. Because they do not have peace, they expect others to tell them that they are right and to give them confirmation. They try to get confirmation in this way because they are not at peace. No one who is independent of the Body ever has real peace. Instead of peace, they have the self.

SELF BEING THE ENEMY OF THE BODY

Seeing the vision of the self has much to do with the Body. Today we are in the Lord's recovery, and the recovery will eventually come to this crucial matter—the building up of the Body. The enemy of the Body is the self. The greatest problem, the greatest frustration and opposition, to the Body is also the self. When we have the self, we do not have the Body. When we have the Body, we do not have the self. In order for the Body to be built up, the self, the independent soul, must be dealt with. The self is the independent "I," the independent "me." When we are independent, we are in the self, the Body is gone, and we do not have peace.

Once again I say that we need the vision of the self. I would urge you to pray about this matter. May the Lord be merciful to us and show us the vision of the self.

CHAPTER FIVE

THE VISION OF THE WORLD

Scripture Reading: 1 John 2:15-17; James 4:4

Let us begin this chapter on the vision of the world by reading two portions of the Word. First John 2:15-17 says, "Do not love the world nor the things in the world. If anyone loves the world, love for the Father is not in him; because all that is in the world, the lust of the flesh and the lust of the eyes and the vainglory of life, is not of the Father but is of the world. And the world is passing away, and its lust, but he who does the will of God abides forever." These verses show us that the world is against God the Father and that the things in the world are against the will of God. James 4:4 also speaks concerning the world: "Adulteresses, do you not know that the friendship of the world is enmity with God? Therefore whoever determines to be a friend of the world is constituted an enemy of God." The world is against God, and those who love the world are enemies of God.

If we would see the vision of the world, we need to have a clear definition of the world. How would you define the term *world*? It is not easy to give an adequate definition.

THE THINGS NEEDED FOR MAN'S EXISTENCE AND THE STEPS OF MAN'S FALL

God created man to live on the earth, and man needs certain things for his existence. In the first chapter of the Bible, two things are mentioned as necessary for man's existence—food and marriage (vv. 29, 28). Man must eat in order to live, and man must marry in order to multiply and replenish the earth. Clothing is not mentioned until the record of the fall of man in chapter three (vv. 7, 10-11, 21).

Immediately after the fall, man sensed that he needed something to cover him. From that time onward clothing has been necessary for man's existence. The first mention of housing in the Bible is in Genesis 4:17. Housing is not mentioned until after the second step of man's fall.

In the fall of man there were three steps. The first step was the fall from the spirit to the soul; the second step was the fall from the soul to the flesh; and the third step was the fall from the flesh to idols. After the first step of the fall, man realized that he was naked, that he was sinful, and thus there was the need of clothing. After the second step of the fall, man became preoccupied with the physical body, and there was the need of housing.

In the garden man and God were on the same level. Then man fell from the spirit to the soul. This means that man fell out of the spirit into the soul. Before the fall man was living mainly by the spirit, but after the first step of the fall, man started to live by the soul, which had been changed into the self. After the first step of the fall, man became sinful, but he was not fleshly, just soulish. After the second step of the fall, the fall from the soul into the flesh, man became fleshly (Gen. 6:3), and this eventually brought in the flood. Finally, in the third step of the fall, which took place after the flood, man fell from the flesh to idols. Man lived not just by the soul and by the flesh but even the more by the idols. By the time of Babel man had fallen to the uttermost and could not become more fallen. Man had fallen from the spirit to the soul, from the soul to the flesh, and from the flesh to idols. Then God came in to call Abraham out of this fall.

What did man need for his existence before the fall? He needed only food and marriage. After the first step of the fall, man became soulish. His understanding was corrupted by sin, he became conscious of evil, and he felt the need for something to cover him. Thus, there was now the need of clothing. Then after the second step of the fall, man began to care mainly for his body and started to build houses for himself. Now man also needed housing.

DELIVERED FROM THE FALL
AND BECOMING SIMPLE

Today, the more people pay attention to their house, the more they are in the fall. In this country a great deal of time, money, and energy are spent on the matter of housing. It takes a lot of time to maintain a modern house. This is a strong sign of being in the fall. I am concerned that even Christians may devote so much time to their house that they have very little, if any, time for prayer. However, the more we are delivered from the fall, the simpler we will become in the matter of housing. When the Lord Jesus was on earth, He could say of Himself, "The foxes have holes, and the birds of heaven have roosts, but the Son of Man has nowhere to lay His head" (Matt. 8:20).

The more fallen we are, the more things we need. On the contrary, the more we are delivered from the fall, the simpler we become regarding what we need for our existence. This is a principle, and we need to keep it in mind. Consider the matter of clothing. Worldly people are occupied with clothing and spend much time and money on their adornment. A saved person, however, should simply care to have clothing that is proper, neat, and clean. The principle is the same with our need for food and transportation. If we look at the life of the Lord Jesus, we will see how simple He was regarding the necessities of human existence.

God agrees that we have all the things that we need for our existence. He has prepared food and the materials for clothing, housing, and transportation. However, there is a limit to what we need.

SATAN CORRUPTING AND SYSTEMATIZING
THE EARTHLY THINGS THAT ARE
NECESSARY FOR HUMAN EXISTENCE

The things that we need for our existence are earthly things, but they are not worldly things. What, then, are the worldly things? Just as the flesh is the corrupted body and the self is the corrupted soul, so the worldly things are the corrupted earthly things. Concerning the origin of the flesh, the self, and the world, the principle is the same.

How were the earthly things corrupted to become the worldly things? The earthly things which are necessary for human existence have been corrupted by Satan with his systematic scheme. Satan has made a system out of all the things which we need for our existence. He has taken the earthly things and has utilized them to make a system. This system includes not only all things but also all people. This means that we have been captured by this system and have become occupied with the things in this system.

PREOCCUPYING ELEMENTS

All the earthly things which are necessary for human existence have become preoccupying elements. For example, we must eat in order to exist, but eating has become a preoccupying element. Likewise, marriage was ordained by God for the existence and multiplication of the human race, but marriage has become a preoccupying element. Originally, clothing was allowed by God for human existence, but eventually clothing became another item utilized by Satan to occupy people. The same is true regarding housing and transportation.

We can become so occupied with these things that there is no ground in us for God. In our human life, there is no time for God. All of our human capacity is preoccupied with and occupied by the things of the world, so no capacity remains in us for God.

The body has been corrupted by the sin of Satan and has become the flesh. The soul has been corrupted by the mind, the thought, of Satan and has become the self. The earthly things have been corrupted by Satan's systematic scheme and have become the world. The world is now a satanic system. In Greek this system is called the *kosmos*. In English this system is called the world.

We all need to have a clear vision of the world. To us the things which we need for our existence may simply be earthly things or they may become a world, a system of Satan. When you are preoccupied with eating, eating becomes an item of the world to you. When you are preoccupied with marriage, marriage becomes an item of the world to you. When you become preoccupied with clothing, housing, and transportation, these also become items of the world to you.

NOT FRUSTRATED FROM THE WILL OF GOD

However, we do not need to be preoccupied with the things we need for our existence. For instance, instead of being preoccupied with food, we may simply use food for us to live for God's purpose. We will then be able to say with Paul, "Foods are for the stomach, and the stomach for foods; but God will bring to nought both it and them" (1 Cor. 6:13a). We are not occupied by eating or preoccupied with eating. The capacity of our human life is not for food—it is for God. To us eating is not an item of the world but merely an item of the earthly things which are necessary for our existence. Eating does not frustrate us from the will of God, and it does not hinder us from realizing God's will.

The situation should be the same with marriage, clothing, housing, and transportation. Marriage is necessary for our existence on earth. We need marriage, but we should not be occupied with marriage. Our marriage should not frustrate us from God's will. If it does, marriage becomes to us an item of the world. Likewise, clothing, housing, and transportation are other necessary items of our earthly life, but if we are preoccupied with these things, they will become items of the world to us.

We are here on earth for God, not for food, marriage, clothing, housing, and transportation. Any of these things that contradicts God's will or hinders God's purpose is an item of the world. None of these things should frustrate us from God's will. If eating does not hinder us from realizing God's will, then for us eating is not an item of the world. Likewise, if marriage does not frustrate us from God's will, then for us marriage is not an item of the world. But once marriage frustrates us from the will of God, it becomes for us an item of the world. If the members of our family hinder us from realizing God's will, then, according to the Lord's word in Luke 14:26, we should hate them. We need to pray that we would see the vision of the world and be delivered from every kind of preoccupation.

DEADENED BY THE FLESH, THE SELF, AND THE WORLD

Man's body became the flesh, man's soul became the self, and the things of the earth were systematized to become the preoccupying world. As a result, man's entire being has been usurped and deadened by Satan. Now there is no possibility for God to accomplish anything for His purpose because man has been deadened by the flesh, the self, and the world.

The human spirit is deadened by the flesh in the body, by the self in the soul, and by the world. The more you live in the flesh and according to the flesh, the more dead you are in your spirit. In like manner, the more you live by the self, the more dead you are in your spirit. Furthermore, living in a worldly way will deaden your spirit. This was our history. Living according to the flesh, by the self, and according to the world, we were deadened in our spirit and were utterly finished with God's purpose.

DELIVERED FROM THE THREE DAMAGING ELEMENTS

The Lord Jesus has come to redeem us, to bring us back to God. He has come to deliver us from the three damaging elements: the flesh, the self, and the world. He begins by quickening, enlivening, our deadened spirit. This means that He has regenerated us, making our spirit alive, and now He dwells in our spirit to be life to us. It is by His being the life within us that we are gradually emancipated, released, and liberated from the flesh, the self, and the world. According to our experience, first we are delivered from the flesh, and then we are gradually delivered from the self. Then, with difficulty, we are delivered from the world.

The deliverance from the flesh, the self, and the world is actually a cycle that is repeated again and again. You may think that you have been thoroughly delivered out of the flesh, the self, and the world. However, you will soon realize that you need a further deliverance from a hidden aspect of the flesh. Thus, you need the liberating Spirit (2 Cor. 3:17) to release you again from the flesh. Following this, you will see that you need the liberating Spirit to release you more from the self and the world. This cycle will be repeated, and with each repetition you will be delivered further from the three elements—the flesh, the self, and the world—which damage humanity as the materials which God created for His building.

Eventually the Lord's recovery will reach the crucial matter of building. If we would realize the building up of the Body, we need to be delivered from the flesh, from the self, and from the world.

NOT CONFORMED TO THIS AGE BUT TRANSFORMED BY THE RENEWING OF THE MIND FOR THE BUILDING UP OF THE BODY

In our experience the liberating Spirit becomes the transforming Spirit (2 Cor. 3:18). The Spirit's liberating work is also the Spirit's transforming work. Eventually we will be transformed into the image of Christ. This is why in Romans 12:2 Paul says, "Do not be fashioned according to this age, but be transformed by the renewing of the mind." To be fashioned according to this age is to be conformed to the present course of the world. Instead of being conformed to the present age, we should be transformed by the renewing of the mind. The more we are transformed, the more we are delivered from the flesh, the self, and the world.

Are you clear about what the world is? Anything can become an item of the world to us, if that thing occupies us and preoccupies us. You need to be fully emancipated from every occupying and preoccupying thing. The time must come when you will be able to say, "Lord, I praise You that I have been liberated. I have been fully emancipated from every kind of preoccupation. On this earth there is nothing occupying me or preoccupying me." When this is your situation, you will have nothing to do with the world, yet you will still be living on the earth. You will continue to need food, marriage, clothing, housing, and transportation, but none of these things will occupy or preoccupy you.

If we see the vision of the world, we will realize that we should not love anything worldly. We should not love any occupying or preoccupying thing. Rather, we should give our love fully, wholly, and absolutely to the Lord. All our capacity is for Him. All the ground, all the room, in us is for Him.

We all need the vision of the world that we may see what the world is and how the enemy uses the world to keep us from realizing the Body. Only when we have been liberated from the world will we be fully built up to realize the Body life.

Chapter Six

THE VISION OF CONSECRATION

Scripture Reading: Acts 1:12-14; Rev. 3:18

In the foregoing chapters we have covered the vision of Christ, the vision of the church, the vision of the Body, the vision of the self, and the vision of the world. In this chapter we need to consider the vision of consecration. As we will see, this vision is of a particular kind of consecration.

BOUND BY THE FLESH, THE SELF, AND THE WORLD

We have pointed out that fallen people are bound by a cord composed of three strands: the flesh, the self, and the world. The flesh is the human body corrupted by the sinful nature of Satan. Sin is nothing less than the sinful nature of Satan injected into the human body, which had been created by God for His purpose. In Romans 6 and 7 sin is personified and likened to a living person who dwells in us, works in us, and reigns in us. As we have the flesh in the body, so we have the self in the soul. The self is the soul plus the satanic mind, the satanic thought.

The human body has become the flesh and the human soul has become the self, but what has happened to the human spirit? There seems to be nothing wrong with the human spirit, for, in contrast to the body and the soul, there is nothing evil or sinful in it. No, there is nothing sinful in the human spirit, but nevertheless the human spirit has been deadened. The spirit has been deadened by the sin in the body and by the self in the soul. The more sinful we are, the more our spirit is deadened. Likewise, the more self-seeking we are, the more our spirit is deadened.

Human beings are bound not only by the flesh and the self but also by the world. Satan has systematized all the things on earth which are necessary for human existence. These things include food, marriage, clothing, housing, and transportation. The Lord provides everything necessary for our existence so that we may live to fulfill His purpose. However, Satan has come in to systematize these things into a system which in the Greek New Testament is called the *kosmos* and in English is called the *world*. Originally all these things were on earth for human existence, and there was nothing wrong with them, but Satan came in to change the earthly things into worldly things. Satan transmuted the human body into the flesh and changed the human soul into the self. In the same principle, Satan has changed the earthly things—the things that were originally on earth for man's existence—into worldly things. These things have become elements of Satan's system, the world, in which all people are imprisoned. Man has been systematized by Satan and has no freedom to fulfill God's purpose.

How evil and how subtle Satan is! Satan has corrupted the human body with sin, causing the body to become the flesh. Satan has polluted the human soul with the satanic mind, causing the soul to become the self. Satan has systematized all the earthly things that are necessary for human existence, organizing them into one system, the world.

THE UNIVERSITY OF THE WORLD

The world may be likened to a large university. A university is a system with many colleges, schools, and departments. In a university there may be a school of medicine, a school of law, a school of business, and a school of liberal arts. Such schools are the systematizing elements of the university. All the students in the university are systematized according to their major, and they study in one of the many schools.

The entire world today is a big "university"—the university of the world. In this university there are different "schools": the school of food, the school of marriage, and the schools of clothing, housing, and transportation. Whereas most students in a university study in just one school, the worldly people, who have been systematized in the university of the world, may study in a number of different schools, taking many "units" at a time but never graduating. They are so busy and so occupied that they have no time for God. They will not say that they are too busy to eat, but they will tell you that they have no time to come to a meeting, to read the Bible, or to pray. They have time for anything in the university of the world, but they have no time for anything related to God.

In the great university of the world, there is also a school of religion. There are even a school of Christianity and a school of Judaism. When the Lord Jesus was on earth, the Jewish people were systematized by Satan in the school of Judaism.

TURNING FROM JUDAISM TO THE HEAVENLY VISION

The apostles and disciples in the early days were taught and trained by the Lord Jesus to realize something new, something absolutely different from Judaism. They came to know Christ, and they saw the vision of Christ. They knew that Christ had been crucified and resurrected, that He had ascended on high, that He had been enthroned and had been made the Lord and Christ, and that He would come back to the earth. They also had the vision of the church and realized that God would gather together His chosen ones and build them up as local churches. They had been in Judaism, but they were turned from Judaism to the heavenly vision.

THE CONSECRATION IN THE UPPER ROOM

Acts 1 speaks of the upper room in Jerusalem. In this upper room a group of about a hundred and twenty prayed for ten days in one accord. They not only prayed, but they also consecrated themselves to the Lord, offering themselves to Him in a very real and practical way.

Three and a half years earlier, the Lord Jesus came to Peter by the seashore, and Peter offered himself to Him. Peter left his job and began to follow the Lord (Matt. 4:18-20). We may say that Peter consecrated himself to the Lord. However, Peter's experience in the upper room was something else. Here Peter had a new kind of consecration, not an ordinary consecration but something specific. At the seashore

Peter gave up his job, indicated by his leaving his fishing nets, but in the upper room he gave up much more. We need to itemize the things Peter gave up in order to be in the upper room.

Standing with the Heavenly Vision
to Give Up the Religion of His Forefathers

The first thing Peter gave up was Judaism. The heavenly vision was contradictory to the religion of his forefathers. Peter's attitude was not to stand with his forefathers' religion but to stand with the heavenly vision. In the first several chapters of Acts, we see that Peter and the other apostles were troubled and persecuted by Judaism, but they continued to take sides with the heavenly vision. The first item of their consecration in the upper room was to give up the traditional religion of their forefathers.

Giving Up His Country

In order to be in the upper room, Peter also gave up his country. Peter was from Galilee, but he left Galilee and came to the upper room in Jerusalem.

Giving Up His Relationships
with His Neighbors and Friends

As a native of Galilee, Peter surely had relationships with his neighbors and friends in Galilee. For Peter to be in the upper room required that he give up these relationships. This is not an insignificant matter. Peter gave up these relationships at a real cost.

Giving Up His Relatives

Peter also gave up his relatives. I doubt whether Peter brought his parents with him into the upper room. There is no hint to this effect. Actually, Peter's parents might have remained in Judaism.

Risking His Life

Finally, Peter was in the upper room at the risk of his life. He was ready to give up his life. At that time Jerusalem was a threatening place to Peter and all the others in the upper room, yet they were willing to risk their lives to be there. In order to be in the upper room, they all gave up Judaism, their country, their neighbors and friends, and their relatives, and they were willing to risk their lives.

THE KIND OF CONSECRATION WE NEED TODAY

We need to see the vision of this upper-room consecration. You may talk much about consecration, but this may be a consecration at the seashore, not a consecration in the upper room. Yes, at the seashore you gave up something to follow the Lord Jesus, but you may not have yet come to the upper room. What kind of consecration do you have—a consecration at the seashore or a consecration in the upper room?

The time in the upper room in Acts 1 was a turning time. It was a time of the turning of an age, a time of the turning of a dispensation. The turn that took place at that time affected heaven and earth. Do you know what the issue of that consecration in the upper room was? That consecration issued in the church. The church came out of the consecration, the dedication, of the one hundred twenty in the upper room.

During those ten days in the upper room, everything was dedicated in a practical way and was dedicated at any cost—at the cost of their forefathers' religion, at the cost of their country, at the cost of their relationships with neighbors and friends, at the cost of their relatives and families, and at the cost of their lives. The only thing they cared for was the heavenly vision. They were "drunken" with this heavenly vision. They were "married" to this heavenly vision; their whole being was held by this heavenly vision; and they were beside themselves with this heavenly vision. This is the kind of consecration we need today.

PAYING THE PRICE FOR THE HEAVENLY VISION

Have you seen the heavenly vision about which we have been speaking? Have you seen the visions of Christ, the church, the Body, the self, and the world? I believe that you have seen something. Will you be able to stand before the Lord at the judgment seat and tell Him that you have not seen any of these visions? Surely you have seen something concerning Christ, the church, the Body, the self, and the world, and thus you are without excuse in this matter.

Some claim that they have not seen the vision. They say this because they are not willing to be in the upper room. In other words, they are not willing to pay the price for the heavenly vision. They know that there is a cost to admitting that they have seen something. They realize that all these visions are costly, but they are not willing to pay the price.

Regarding this matter of cost, or price, let us read the word of the Lord Jesus in Revelation 3:18: "I counsel you to buy from Me gold refined by fire that you may be rich, and white garments that you may be clothed and that the shame of your nakedness may not be manifested, and eyesalve to anoint your eyes that you may see." In this verse the Lord counsels us not to pray nor to ask nor to receive nor to take by faith; He counsels us to *buy*. Here we are concerned only with the third of the three things which the Lord counsels us to buy—eyesalve to anoint our eyes that we may see. Perhaps, in a sense, you have not seen the heavenly vision, but as soon as you are willing to pay the price, to buy the eyesalve, you will see. The crucial matter is the willingness to pay the price. Once you come into the upper room, everything is clear. But if you are not willing to come into the upper room, no matter how many messages you hear, you still will not be able to see.

You need to buy the eyesalve. Do not excuse yourself by saying that you have not seen the vision. Do not say that you are not clear. You may be clear, but you may not be willing to pay the price. If you are not willing to pay the price, you will not dare to say that you have seen the vision. Whether or not you have seen the vision depends on this one matter— whether you are willing to pay the price. Pay the price to buy the eyesalve and you will see the vision.

I encourage you to pray, saying, "Lord Jesus, by Your mercy I will buy the eyesalve. By Your mercy I am willing to pay the price to be in the upper room." If you say this to the Lord, the heavens will be opened, the scales will fall from your eyes, and you will see the heavenly vision.

BURNING THE BRIDGES BEHIND US

If you pay the price for the heavenly vision, you will "burn the bridges" behind you and will have no way to go backward. Christianity will be behind you, and you will have no way to return to it. Even if you wanted to go back, the people would not accept you.

However, suppose that one day an offer is presented to you, an opportunity to have a better position or a better future. The opportunity may be for you, or it may be for your wife or children. Would you consider this offer? For you to consider such an offer would mean that you have not burned all the bridges. It would mean that you have left yourself a way to go back. By the Lord's mercy I can testify that I burned all my bridges more than thirty years ago. We should not be ashamed of burning our bridges—we should praise the Lord for it.

THE COST OF TAKING THE WAY
OF THE LORD'S RECOVERY

To take the way of the Lord's recovery is not cheap. This way is expensive; it requires a costly consecration. To take this way will be at the cost of the religion of your fathers and of your country, at the cost of your relationships with your neighbors and of your relatives, and at the cost of your own life. Are you ready for such a consecration? Are you ready to come in the upper room to be clear concerning the heavenly vision?

We are here not for a movement but for the Lord's recovery. How can the recovery be realized? The recovery can be realized, carried out, only by the experience of the consecration in the upper room. This is not an ordinary consecration; it is a special consecration, a specific consecration, an extraordinary consecration. This consecration is a turning point.

What happened to those one hundred and twenty who were in the upper room in Acts 1? They all became a burnt offering. They were burning and they burned others. We also need to be burned, and then we will burn others.

What are you expecting today? Do you expect a revival or a movement? Do you expect a new kind of Christian activity?

What are we doing here? Have we come together to hear something that we cannot hear elsewhere? We may be here for this reason, but this is not enough. We must be here for the Lord's recovery, which is the issue of an upper-room consecration.

IN THE CROWD OR IN THE UPPER ROOM?

When the Lord Jesus was on earth, great crowds followed Him. Multitudes were saved and healed, and multitudes received the favor of God. Eventually, however, there were only about one hundred and twenty in the upper room. The crowds, the multitudes, did not afford the Lord Jesus anything for His move. The Lord's move was with those in the upper room, with those whose eyes had been opened and whose hearts had been touched. This small number came into the upper room to be burned, and then they turned the whole world upside down. The principle is the same today. It is a small number who will turn the world and change the age.

Do you intend to be in the crowd or in the upper room? Will you remain one of the multitude, or by the Lord's mercy will you come into the upper room? I do not know who you are. Only the Lord knows who will be in the upper room.

I would urge you to pray to receive the Lord's mercy that you might be in the upper room. If you are not willing to come here, then what you have read in these chapters will have nothing to do with you. Then you will be like those in the crowds, those the Lord did not count on. If you would be in the upper room, you need to pray in a specific way and say, "Lord, I am willing to be in the upper room for the recovery of Your testimony."